AF448258

hey there little critters

BY: MELISSA WHITTINGTON

THIS BOOK IS FOR WOLFIE,
WHO LOVES TO USE HIS NEW
WORDS.

I see a monkey swinging in the tree.
Who's that monkey staring at me?

Butterfly,
Butterfly, in
the sky.
How many
butterflies
can you find?

Some say
they buzz.
Some say
they sing.
Can you make
the sound of
a bumble
bees wings?

The trees stand tall as they can be. Do you like to look up at a tree?

The turtle walks slow. Like there's nowhere to go.

Oh, little caterpillar don't you cry. One day you'll become a butterfly.

Little orange fish

in the sea.

How many of
you can
there be?

Hello grasshopper. How are you?
I wish I could jump that high too!

Hey there
baby bird.
Tweet Tweet
Tweet.
What will
mama bird
bring to eat?

Here's a
Ladybug
Red and Black.
How many
spots are on its
back?

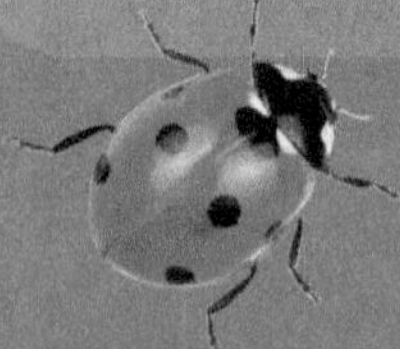

On a lily pad,
the frog does
sit.
It never sinks
and its the
perfect fit.

Be careful there's a snake. Its over by the lake.

Panda in bamboo,
black and white.
Munching on leaves
What a sight!

There's an alligator
Hiding in the swamp.
He likes to go
Chomp
Chomp
Chomp!

The green
gecko
likes to
crawl.
When he
sees bugs
He eats them
all.

Good
Bye

www.ingramcontent.com/pod-product-compliance
Lightning Source LLC
Chambersburg PA
CBHW050818160726
48004CB00002B/895